THE PRESBYTERIAN DEACON

Other titles of interest

Presbyterian Polity for Church Leaders
Fourth edition
Joan S. Gray and Joyce C. Tucker

The Presbyterian Ruling Elder
Paul S. Wright
Revised by Stephens G. Lytch

Sailboat Church:
Helping Your Church Rethink Its Mission and Practice
Joan S. Gray

Selected to Serve:
A Guide for Church Leaders
Second edition
Earl S. Johnson, Jr.

Spiritual Leadership for Church Officers:
A Handbook
Joan S. Gray

To order these books, visit our Web site at
www.pcusastore.com or call 1-800-533-4371.

THE PRESBYTERIAN DEACON

AN ESSENTIAL GUIDE

Earl S. Johnson, Jr.

WESTMINSTER
JOHN KNOX PRESS
LOUISVILLE • KENTUCKY

Revised edition
Published by Westminster John Knox Press
Louisville, Kentucky

21 22 23 24 25 26 27 28 29 30—10 9 8 7 6 5 4 3 2

Book design by Sharon Adams
Cover design by Night & Day Design

Library of Congress Cataloging-in-Publication Data is on file at the
Library of Congress, Washington, DC.

ISBN-13: 978-0-664-26808-4

Most Westminster John Knox Press books are available at special
quantity discounts when purchased in bulk by corporations, organizations, and special-interest groups. For more information,
please e-mail SpecialSales@wjkbooks.com.

Contents

Preface to the Second Edition

Since the editors of Geneva Press originally asked me to write an introduction to the work of the deacons in the Presbyterian Church (U.S.A.) in 2000, a great many changes have taken place in the church as a whole and in our denomination in particular.

In the summer of 2011, for example, the General Assembly, after the requisite endorsement of the majority of presbyteries, approved a new *Book of Order* that created revised standards for ordained ministry (called "ordered ministry"). Not only was the title "minister" changed to "teaching elder," but the church decided to endow our constitution with "a new openness to God's mission in the world" (F-1.0404), a new energy, and a new flexibility that all make it possible "to see both the possibilities and perils of institutional form in order to ensure the faithfulness of these forms to God's activity in the world." Those who want to see a more detailed exploration of what being a church leader means today (and in the future) can see my book *Selected to Serve: A Guide for Church Leaders*, 2nd ed. (Louisville, KY: Geneva Press, 2012).

As a consequence, the description of the work of the deacons has been considerably abbreviated (G-2.02), and many of the previous guidelines are gone. Some of them have been absorbed into directives about what teaching elders, ruling elders, and deacons all should do (see G-2.04 for example).

In many ways this reduction is healthy and necessary for the future work of deacons in our denomination. Most Presbyterians know how much the church and our culture have changed in the last few years. Many congregations are struggling to survive. All our churches are working to figure out what the meaning of ministry must be in the future in order to continue to witness to Jesus Christ and provide service in his name to coming generations that may not value Presbyterianism and previous styles of worship as much as their predecessors did. The fact that deacons have a shorter job description gives us the flexibility we need to respond to new opportunities and challenges and forces us to assess our weaknesses as well as our strengths. But it also makes us more and more dependent on the Holy Spirit to guide us and give us creativity, insight, and perspicacity to try, discard, and strengthen new types of diaconal and pastoral ministries.

It is necessary to mention another significant alteration in our polity that potentially influences the work of deacons. In 2011, after years of discussion and debate that began in

1973, the church decided to permit the ordination of gays and lesbians as deacons, ruling elders, and teaching elders. Since all Presbyterians, regardless of sexual orientation, are now eligible to serve in ordered ministry, some congregations may discover that many men and women, once disqualified, are now available to use their gifts. It is to be hoped that their presence will enrich Christ's work, not only in the local church family but in the whole community in which the congregation resides.

Writing a second edition of guidelines for deacons is a welcome challenge since it calls us all to look afresh at an important part of our ministry together and think carefully and prayerfully about what it must become while keeping in mind, at the same time, the deep biblical and historical roots of diaconal ministry. Therefore with one foot in the past and the other in the future, let us step boldly into this new adventure, confident that God will lead us wherever we need to go. I explore some of the new possibilities for ministry in detail in the last chapter.

As discussed at the beginning of the first edition, we are endeavoring to strengthen a ministry that is first in the church in many ways:

- the first ordered ministry many church members assume;
- the first major commitment they make to the work of the wider church; and
- the first organized experience they have in taking part in the caring work of the congregation.

This book has been kept short deliberately in order to make it as useful as possible. A new deacon should be able to read it in one or two sittings to get a quick overview of the responsibilities now and a foretaste of what may be required in the years ahead. Those who have been deacons for some time will also find it useful as it explores the implications of a diaconal ministry based on a new, more flexible church polity.

Earl S. Johnson, Jr.
Johnstown, New York
September 2012

UPDATE TO SECOND EDITION
This revision reflects changes in the Constitution, particularly in the Directory for Worship and the *Book of Confessions*. The Directory was rewritten, and the Belhar Confession was added in 2016. In addition, the title "teaching elder" was changed back to "minister of the Word and Sacrament."

Earl S. Johnson, Jr.
April 2020

Introduction

For those who love people and want to follow in the ministry of Jesus Christ, there is no better office to assume than that of deacon in the Presbyterian Church (U.S.A.). As the *Book of Order* puts it, "The ministry of deacon as set forth in Scripture is one of compassion, witness, and service, sharing in the redeeming love of Jesus Christ for the poor, the hungry, the sick, the lost, the friendless, the oppressed, those burdened by unjust policies or structures, or anyone in distress. Persons of spiritual character, honest repute, exemplary lives, brotherly and sisterly love, sincere compassion, and sound judgment should be chosen for this ministry."

Traditionally, deacons are people persons. Their hearts go out to those in distress: to members who have suffered loss; to neighbors in the hospital; to friends who have lost their jobs; to new parents who are confused by a wonderful, sudden, and challenging change in the responsibilities of life; to new members who need a word of welcome; to members who are shut in and lonely and cannot leave their homes; to people in the community who have lost their way and can no longer find God; to those who are economically oppressed and do not have adequate places to live or enough to eat; to those suffering from natural disasters or the ravages of war; to any people who need to experience the love of Christ in concrete ways.

Clearly deacons are not the only Presbyterians who provide these ministries of sympathy and caring. All Christians are charged to love their neighbors and care for one another. But the deacons provide an *organized* way of bringing the love of Jesus Christ to the church and the community. Deacons, by assisting the pastor(s) in pastoral care, by working closely with the session to bring justice to the village, town, or city in which they live, by taking seriously the admonition to love one another from the heart (1 Pet. 1:22), fulfill the command of Jesus to "love one another as I have loved you" (John 15:12) in ways for the whole world to experience and see.

The *Book of Order* makes it clear that deacons do more than provide simple acts of caring and concern, as important as they are in a rushed and frantic society. The Constitution of the Presbyterian Church (U.S.A.) calls the whole church, and especially the deacons, to go beyond giving love merely to those we know, or those who ask for help, but to become "a community of hope," "a community of love," and "a community of witness" to the whole world (F-1.0301). If being compassionate goes beyond loving those who love us, or who are related to us, to the showing of a deep, sympathizing love to all the children of God, then it calls deacons to the kind of love described in the New Testament as *agape* (Matt. 24:12; Luke 11:42; John 13:35; 15:9; Rom. 5:5; 8:39), to the love we see in the ministry, death, and resurrection of Jesus Christ. This love puts the other first and wants to serve rather than be served (Mark 10:45). It gives totally of itself, beyond all measure or asking. The love of Christ in us is the highest and greatest of all—patient, open, trustworthy, hopeful, enduring, and being so grounded finally in the plan of God. It can even be called eternal (1 Cor. 13), because it is of God (1 John 4:7–12).

This book is itself a work of love. It has been my privilege to work with deacons in four different churches in New York State, and I have learned to appreciate their open hearts, their willingness to dirty their hands, their high sense of calling, and their warm and friendly smiles. It is to the deacons in West Charlton, Plattsburgh, Pittsford, and Johnstown that I dedicate this book, with thanks for all they have taught and given me.

For new deacons, for those who are working to energize the work of the diaconate in their church, or for those who are considering the call to become a deacon, I hope that the enthusiasm I feel for this important work of compassion, witness, and service will be catching. Now is not a time to become discouraged or disheartened about deacons' work, when the world so desperately needs more, not fewer, acts of love in the name of Jesus Christ. God definitely calls us through the agency of the Holy Spirit to a ministry of service, caring, and justice. Let us open our hearts and minds to respond to the call when it comes our way, knowing that all things are possible in the grace of God and the love of Jesus. May all of us be re-rooted in Christ's love so that the Spirit will enable us to comprehend how much power is available to "accomplish abundantly far more than all we can ask or imagine" (Eph. 3:17–21).

Chapter 1

The Biblical Background

After the positions of apostle and elder, the ordered ministry of deacon was one of the first ones established by the New Testament church. According to Acts 6, the early Christians faced an enviable problem of church growth. Disciples were increasing in number, and the Hellenists (Greek-speaking Christians, in contrast to those who came from an Aramaic or Hebrew background) complained that their people were being shortchanged in a ministry that had been established to distribute food. The twelve disciples of Jesus (by this time Judas Iscariot had been replaced by Matthias; see Acts 1:23–26) called a meeting of the church leaders, and it was decided that a new group of seven should be chosen to "wait on tables" (*diakonein trapezais*) so that the others could continue in the work of preaching and praying. It is not a coincidence that all of the first deacons (*diakonoi*) had Greek names. Obviously it was true already in the first century: if you complain, you get the job! The fact that the leader of the initial group of deacons (Stephen) was stoned to death for teaching and preaching demonstrates that at the start the church had more in mind for them than menial tasks.

It is an interesting phenomenon that the early church decided to give one of its most important groups of church officers a mundane, commonplace name. In the modern world we would no doubt want people to feel important in their new position and give them a dignified title, something like Social Service Provider or Caring Minister. But the church chose the title *diakonos,* which, in its most literal sense, means a person who serves food to other people in a home or a restaurant, perhaps even akin to "slave." Since their duties required them to meet the needs of others, even washing the feet of travelers, it was not always the most enviable of jobs.

Why did the early church choose such a humble title for their new leaders? Obviously they took it from the ministry and example of Jesus Christ, who taught his disciples that if anyone wants to be first in the kingdom of God, he or she has to be the servant of all (Mark 9:35). Jesus followed the example of the Suffering Servant in Isaiah, the one who would be exalted and lifted up (Isa. 52:13) by being wounded for the transgressions of others (Isa. 53). This servant Jesus knew was not a sycophant, or one who curried the favor of others to get ahead, but the afflicted one who bore the sin of many.

It is one in whom God delights, and because God's Spirit is in him, or her, brings forth justice to the nations (Isa. 42:1). The servant of the Lord does not call attention to himself or herself, but to God who has commanded the service:

> You are my witnesses, says the LORD, and my servant whom I have chosen, so that you may know and believe me and understand that I am he. Before me no god was formed, nor shall there be any after me. I, I am the LORD, and besides me there is no savior. (Isa. 43:10–11)

The Gospels tell us repeatedly that Jesus called attention to the exalted status that comes from service:

- Those who want to be great among you must be your servant. (Mark 10:43, au. paraphr.)
- "For the Son of Man came not to be served but to serve, and to give his life a ransom for many." (Mark 10:45)
- Whoever serves me must follow me, and where I am, there will my servant be also. Whoever serves me, God will honor. (John 12:26, au. paraphr.)
- "Servants are not greater than their master, nor are messengers greater than the one who sent them." (John 13:16; see Matt. 10:24; Luke 6:40)

The earliest written reference in the New Testament to the ordered ministry of deacons (*diaconoi*) is found in Phil. 1:1 where Paul greets them with the bishops (*episkopoi*). A later writer (1 Tim. 3:8–13) provides the first list of personal

qualifications that were required of deacons. They must do
the following:

- Be tested by the church.
- Be bold in faith, holding fast to the mystery of faith.
- Be good managers of their own households (see the
  requirements for bishops: 3:4–5).
- Be capable of sustaining long-term relationships.
- Be committed and serious minded.
- Be honest, not double-tongued.
- Have no addictive personality traits, "not indulging
  in much wine" (see a more detailed discussion of
  all these requirements in chapter 3).

In return, the deacons will receive at least two major
rewards:

- good standing for themselves and meaningful service and
- the privilege of following Jesus' example (see
  G-3.0102).

Throughout the New Testament, service to God (*diakonia*) is considered to be a central characteristic of those dedicated to being Jesus' disciples. Paul indicates that beyond
the fact that Stephen was one of the first deacons, his whole
family "devoted themselves to the service of the saints"
(1 Cor. 16:15). For the early Christians, several spiritual

traits were all bound together: "love, faith, service, and patient endurance" (Rev. 2:19). As Paul puts it in a well-known passage in 1 Cor. 12:4–6, "Now there are varieties of gifts, but the same Spirit; and there are varieties of services, but the same Lord; and there are varieties of activities, but it is the same God who activates all of them in everyone." The different gifts (*charismata*), services (δ*iakoniōn*), and action items (*energēmatōn*) all provide energy, enthusiasm, and power for the church "for the common good." Deacons and other leaders are not called to suit themselves or to make themselves look good, but only to serve the Lord and the unity of the one church, for the purpose of interpreting the faith, healing the sick, prophesying, or providing spiritual discernment. God appoints different people to perform various tasks within the church (see a list in 1 Cor. 12:27–31), but the things they have in common are orders from the same God and the same desire to serve the body of Christ. Service is a characteristic not just of the deacon but of the apostle (Rom. 11:13; 2 Cor. 4:1; 6:3–4; Acts 1:17, 25), the evangelist, or the mission worker (2 Tim. 4:5), and even angels (Heb. 1:14: "Are not all angels spirits in the divine service, sent to serve for the sake of those who are to inherit salvation?"). It is a requirement of anyone who follows Jesus.

Although the admonition given to one Archippus in Col. 4:17 could apply to us all—"See that you complete the task [literally *service*] that you have received in the Lord"—the work given by God through Jesus Christ was not considered by the first Christians to be an onerous chore. It was a "ministry" (NRSV; in Greek, *diaconia*) "of the Spirit come in glory," "a ministry of justification [righteousness] bound in glory" (2 Cor. 3:7–11), a ministry of forgiveness and reconciliation (2 Cor. 5:18–19), a ministry of generosity to the saints (2 Cor. 9:1, 12–13); it was, above all, a service of love, for indeed love is the highest of all the duties and gifts that God bestows (1 Cor. 13:13). Deacons may do a variety of things in many different congregations, but if they are not filled with the greatest gift to serve the greatest God, then they and their ministry will probably amount to nothing. Paul urges us all to pursue our callings with the utmost of energy and compassion. Let us use our gifts according to the grace given to us: prophecy in proportion to our faith; teaching in relation to our ability to teach; preaching in sermon delivery; giving and stewardship in generosity; ministry (*diakonian*) in serving (*diakonia*); and giving mercy and forgiveness in the absolute cheerfulness and abandonment of love (Rom. 12:6–8).

Questions for Study and Reflection

1. Read Acts 6:1–7. Can you see how the distribution of food to the hungry is to be considered an act of love given by God? What are the qualities that the disciples looked for in the first deacons? What does it mean to be "of good

standing, full of the Spirit and of wisdom" (v. 3)? Do you see some of these traits in the members of your board of deacons?

2. Look at the qualifications required for deacons in 1 Tim. 3:8–13. Do you have all eight of them? Are there any you have to work on? Do you need to ask God to give you some of them?

3. What is meant in 1 Pet. 4:11 where it says that "whoever serves must do so with the strength that God supplies, so that God may be glorified in all things through Jesus Christ?" Is God strengthening you in your ministry as a deacon? Can you feel God's power in the life of your church? What can you do as deacons where the congregation's ministry is weak?

Chapter 2

Deacons in the Reformed Tradition and the Presbyterian Church

Men and Women as Deacons

*W*hen Presbyterians examine the background of the role of deacons in the Reformed tradition, it is not surprising that they discover that the influence of the reformer John Calvin has been substantial. In his *Institutes of the Christian Religion* and his commentaries on the Bible, Calvin carefully explained his understanding of the biblical concept of the diaconate and the way it should function in the church.[1]

In the *Institutes*, for example, Calvin makes it clear that the primary task of the deacons is to take care of the poor and distribute alms. He had made a careful study of the way deacons functioned in the Roman Catholic Church and

---

1. For a detailed history of the background of the office in Calvin's Geneva and in later years, see the excellent study by Elsie Anne McKee, *Diakonia in the Classical Reformed Tradition and Today* (Grand Rapids: W. B. Eerdmans Publishing Co., 1989).

was harshly critical that no more of the money for the poor reached those for whom it was intended than if it had been thrown into the sea (4.5.15). Frequently deacons merely functioned as liturgical and administrative assistants to bishops and priests, and too often they abused their office. When people misuse or steal money that has been given for a sacred purpose, Calvin contends, they mock the church with a false diaconate. The diaconate, he charges, was never established to create a license to steal and rob or to turn a ministry into sacrilegious plundering (4.5.16).

In Geneva, Calvin organized the work of the deacons into two different branches. Based on his interpretation of the New Testament, and in response to a welfare system already established in the city that had church leaders and civic employees both working with the disadvantaged, he created one group to manage and distribute the money collected, and a second to do the actual work of caring for the sick and poor (4.3.9). This bifurcation of responsibilities was partially based on his exegesis of Rom. 12:8 and 1 Tim. 5:9–10. Seeing that there were different types of ministries established in the Pauline churches, Calvin decided that one group should have administrative authority for the caring ministry of the church and that the other should do the hands-on work.

No doubt Calvin's organization of the ministry to the poor derived from a deep commitment to the teaching and example of Jesus. In his discussion of Christian freedom, he urges his readers not to let their use of good things lead to gluttony and luxury (3.19.9) or to neglect of the weak (3.19.10). Anyone the Christian meets, Calvin writes, even if a stranger, is not a person who can be refused help. How can we say that anyone is ugly who has been given the image of God? A believer cannot argue that helping the poor is not worth the effort. For Calvin, it is worth every-thing, even giving yourself and all your possessions (3.7.6). This kind of perspective has guided followers of Jesus Christ before and since, and in this Calvin provides a model worth emulating.

Calvin's division of labor in the church's ministry to the poor into two separate parts, however, is another question since he decided that men, and only men, should take on the first task of administration and control and that women should assume the second job of providing them actual care. He justified this split arrangement of responsibilities partially on the basis of his understanding of Scripture and partially on common cultural assumptions. For Calvin, even though he truly had compassion for the poor, it was unthinkable that women would have any kind of power or control over men. In his view, women, even if they held office in the church, were subordinate, and had been since the time Adam and Eve were created. Because women were born to obey (1 Tim. 2:12), he gave men the dominant role as deacons, and women the more subservient position. Even though he acknowledged that Paul commended Phoebe as a deacon of the church in Cenchreae (probably one of the two ports of Corinth) in Rom. 16:1, Calvin denied that she was a leader functioning with the same authority as men. Instead, he incorrectly linked this passage with the description of the work of older widows in 1 Tim. 5:9–10, who had been given responsibility for charity in the church, and concluded that Phoebe was also assigned this important but secondary role of caring for the sick, having no administrative or ecclesiastical responsibility.

Unfortunately, Calvin provided the rationale for a system that perpetuated itself for several hundred years: a deep commitment to the underprivileged[2] linked with a blind spot that made it possible to overlook the degradation of women who were forced to become deaconesses or auxiliary deacons in the performance of a church office they once held equally with men. It is likely that a similar attitude obtained in later church history when other people were excluded from ministry on the basis of race, wealth, or social standing.

Not much changed in the Reformed churches until the end of the 1800s and the beginning of the twentieth century. Generally it was agreed that women should remain silent in the churches and be subordinate to male authority. The situation did not begin to shift until the period after women participated in the abolitionist and women's suffrage move-

2. See statements in The Second Helvetic Confession, C-5.117; The Confession of 1967, C-46; A Brief Statement of Faith, C-10.2.

ments prior to the Civil War. In the latter part of the nineteenth century, women began to take a part in mission organizations on local and denominational levels. As the church began to develop a new understanding of the Bible, largely due to the advent of modern higher criticism, demands began to surface for the equality of women in ministry. It was not until 1906, however, that women became deacons in the United Presbyterian Church of North America. In 1915 they were allowed to be elected as deaconesses in a manner similar to that appointed for deacons in the PCUSA. In 1921 they obtained the full privileges of the diaconate in the Cumberland Presbyterian Church, but it was not until 1923 that both men and women could serve together in the UPCUSA. The privilege of equality in ministry was not extended to women as elders until 1930, however, and women were not finally approved as ministers of the Word and Sacrament until 1956 (UPCUSA) and 1965 (PCUS).[3]

Today, the situation is much different. While the election to ordered ministry is decided by the local congregation and no one can be placed in ordered ministry except by vote of that body (G-2.0102, F-3.0106), the Constitution also makes it clear that there can be no discrimination in the selection of members, ministers, deacons, or trustees. The church

---

3. A detailed discussion of this struggle is provided in Lois A. Boyd and R. Douglas Brackenridge, *Presbyterian Women in America: Two Centuries of a Quest for Status,* 2nd ed. (Westport, Conn.: Greenwood Press, 1996).

is charged with the responsibility of working toward greater inclusiveness in its corporate life. "This unity of believers in Christ is reflected in the rich diversity of the Church's membership. In Christ, by the power of the Spirit, God unites persons through baptism regardless of race, ethnicity, age, sex, disability, geography, or theological conviction. There is therefore no place in the life of the Church for discrimination against any person. The Presbyterian Church (U.S.A.) shall guarantee full participation and representation in its worship, governance, and emerging life to all persons or groups within its membership. No member shall be denied participation or representation for any reason other than those stated in this Constitution" (F-1.0403; also see F-1.0404; G-1.0302; 3.0103).

Differing Roles of Deacons
in the Presbyterian Church

Many Presbyterians may not realize that the role of deacons differs in various parts of the country and that some congregations do not have a board of deacons at all.[4] The *Book of Order allows* churches to have a board of deacons, but it does not *require* deacons as it mandates ruling elders

---

4. A history of different uses of the board of deacons in various streams of the Presbyterian Church in the United States is provided by Joan S. Gray and Joyce C. Tucker, *Presbyterian Polity for Church Leaders,* 4th ed. (Louisville, Ky.: Geneva Press, 2012), 39–46.

and a session. "A congregation by a majority vote may choose not to utilize the ordered ministry of deacons. If the congregation has neither a board of deacons nor individually commissioned deacons, the function of this ordered ministry shall be the responsibility of the ruling elders and the session" (G-2.0202).

What is more, the board of deacons may be structured in one or both of two different ways (G-2.0202):

1. They may be organized as a board with the pastor, copastors, or associate pastors, as advisory members. (The pastors may participate in the meetings but cannot vote.) In such a case, the deacons may elect a moderator and a secretary from among their own membership, and they take primary responsibility for running meetings and enabling the board to develop short- and long-term mission statements and goals, as well as annual budgets to be approved by the session. The structure of administration of each board, under the current Form of Government, is to be determined by each congregation in its by laws or by the individual board or committee.

2. Deacons may also be individually commissioned by the session to particular tasks consistent with the responsibilities of their ordered ministry. Presumably deacons could be asked to take on the care of shut-ins, the poor in the congregation, and others in need, or could be empowered to become the chairpersons of special committees charged with these and other tasks. The Form of Government

particularly mentions "caring for members in need, handling educational tasks, cultivating liberality in giving, collecting and disbursing monies to specific persons or causes, or overseeing the buildings and property of the congregation." In small churches where it is difficult to find enough leaders to staff a board or members do not have the time or are too far apart to meet regularly, this kind of arrangement could facilitate the ongoing ministry of the congregation. See chapter 6 for more possibilities.

Regardless of the organizational plan chosen, the session and the deacons must remain in constant communication so that the congregation's goals and the requirements of the *Book of Order* are achieved. In many congregations, one of the deacons (often the moderator) is invited to attend stated session meetings so that information can flow in both directions. The deacons may also be given the opportunity to report regularly to the congregation through the church newsletter, through mission announcements in services of worship, or through special services when the work of the diaconate is recognized and explained. (See the Litany in this book's appendix.) Deacons may also be appointed to work on other committees or to serve as trustees.

The work of deacons is not limited only to those elected and ordained to that specific ordered ministry. Some churches may have so much work in the community and the congregation that the board may not be able to accomplish all that is required even if it has forty members or more. In such cases, the deacon may assume other duties delegated to him or her by the session (G-2.0202).

Congregations may also differ considerably in regard to the responsibilities of the board of deacons once they are established. Traditionally, before unification in 1983, the southern church (PCUS) used a model in which the deacons were given fiscal duties like those assumed by trustees in other parts of the church. In the northern church (UPCUSA), they focused more on the biblical requirements of sympathy, witness, and service.

An examination of the function of deacons across the country and the call by the 204th General Assembly (1992) for more flexibility and creativity in the performance of their ministry within the Reformed tradition will be considered in chapter 6.[5]

Questions for Study and Reflection

1. Can you find out how long your congregation has had a board of deacons? Do you know what their original responsibilities were?

---

5. "Theology and Practice of Ordination in the Presbyterian Church (U.S.A.)," in General Assembly Minutes (Louisville, Ky.: Office of the General Assembly, 1992), 1021–92.

2. How long have women served on the board? Do you know who the first woman was to be ordained as a deacon or ruling elder?

3. In your board of deacons, which one of the responsibilities listed in chapter 2 of the *Book of Order* is the most important? Which one is the least significant?

4. How does your nominating committee search for new deacons? What kind of experiences, commitments, and personality traits do you require? Do you have any high school or college students serving on your board?

Chapter 3

Who Are the Deacons and What Do They Do?

Election and Relationship to the Congregation

*D*eacons, ruling elders, and trustees are all chosen by the congregation of the local church in the same manner. Each year the congregation elects a nominating committee (usually at the annual meeting), which is assigned the task of recommending names in the following year to fill vacancies in ordered ministry. The composition of the committee is to be determined by each congregation, providing that it is "drawn from and representative of its membership" (G-2.0401). At least one member of the committee must be a ruling elder chosen by the session and at least three other members must be elected by the congregation. Each deacon or ruling elder is elected for a period of three years (unless the person is filling an unexpired term) and is normally eligible to be elected for one more three-year term (G-2.0404). Any deacon or ruling elder serving for a total of six consecutive years cannot be elected to the same ordered ministery again until a year has passed. It is also possible for a congregation to decide that leaders are ineligible for reelection after only one term of service.

Although ruling elders and deacons are elected by the congregation and are responsible to the members of the church, the session has the authority to examine people chosen to be elders and deacons to determine their willingness to serve and their suitability for ordered ministry. All sessions do not exercise this power, but it is possible to conduct a period of study and preparation, including an examination of the candidates' personal faith and their knowledge of their constitutional duties. If the candidates are approved, the session sets a date for ordination. The vows that deacons take during the ordination service are discussed in chapter 4.

Relationship to the Session

The authority of the session to direct the work of the board of deacons is not confined simply to the election process. Since the session is the ruling body of the church, the deacons do not have independent power, even though they may function on their own once church policies have been approved. The session is responsible for the mission and government of a particular church and has the responsibility to delegate and supervise the work of the board of deacons (G-3.0201c) and all other organizations within the congregation, "leading the congregation in participating in the mission of the whole church" (G-3.0201c). Generally all records of the board of deacons must be submitted to the session at least once a year, and the session has the power to overrule or change any action the board may take or to direct it to reconsider such action.

In most congregations, the relationship between the session and the deacons remains a harmonious one, as long as good communication between the two groups is maintained (see the discussion in chapter 1) and as long as ruling elders and deacons understand and respect the constitutional responsibilities of both boards. The Form of Government used to require an annual joint meeting of the two boards to confer on "matters of common interest" (G-6.0405 in 2009/2011 *Book of Order*) that allow ruling elders and deacons to share their main concerns, their frustrations, and their hopes and dreams for the future. If at all times leaders and members are committed to Jesus Christ and remember that the work accomplished is mission in his name, if they pray and work constantly for cooperation and for guidance by the Holy Spirit, and if they avoid the temptation to make decisions for the purpose of personal power plays and believe that all members are called to serve rather than be served, it is likely that mutual esteem will be maintained and that the two boards will be enabled to function together like two hands that serve the one body of Christ.

What is said about the responsibilities of councils in the *Book of Order* applies to all members of the church: "The mutual interconnection of the church through its councils is a sign of the unity of the church. . . . All councils of the church are united by the nature of the church and share with one another responsibilities, rights, and powers as provided in this Constitution. The councils are distinct, but have such mutual relations that the act of any one of them is the act of the whole church" (G-3.0101).

Relationship to the Pastor(s)

Normally, if the deacons function together as a board, the pastor or one or more of the associate or co-pastors serve as "advisory members." Although a pastor has the right to speak at all meetings, he or she is not able to vote.

Because deacons and ruling elders and pastors share many responsibilities in common, pastors (along with the ruling elders) are to exercise pastoral care and exhibit special concern for the poor, the sick, the troubled, and the dying. "With the deacons they are to share in the ministries of compassion, witness, and service" (G-2.0504). Usually the pastor who is working with the board of deacons meets regularly with the moderator to determine meeting agendas, maintain communication with the session and congregation, develop short- and long-range plans, and, with the deacons' secretary or treasurer, monitor the deacons' annual budget.

Responsibilities

The board of deacons might be described most generally as "the caring arm of the church." Although all members are called by Jesus Christ to love their neighbors and give the cup of cold water to the stranger, most congregations need an *organized* ministry of compassion so that those in need are not overlooked. Most Americans are incredibly busy, and even church members may forget to regard one another with genuine concern and love. It is a regrettable fact that in churches of all sizes, people can be absent from worship without being missed or can go through an illness or family tragedy without getting the comfort and attention they need. Congregants can experience financial problems, lose a job, or be deprived of the value of an investment because a stock crashes or an employer misuses retirement funds, without others even knowing about such crises. Leaders and friends may not have enough information to make sure that the affected family's basic needs (payment of bills, provision of health insurance, groceries, etc.) are being met. At such times, it is often necessary for the deacons to step forward in an organized way to marshal the love and concern of the whole congregation to help members endure pain and tragedy. All members, along with the deacons, must be vigilant to be prayerfully concerned about the needs of people in the church and take care not to fall into the trap of being so interested in friends and neighbors or the pressing work of the congregation that they ignore those in need who are in worship every Sunday morning.

In most churches, this primary line of caring defense is the way deacons understand their role of "compassion, witness, and service, sharing in the redeeming love of Jesus Christ." Chapter G-2.02 of the *Book of Order* describes the work of the deacons briefly without giving details about how the ministry should be carried out. Particularly they should care "for the poor, the hungry, the sick, the lost, the friendless, the oppressed, those burdened by unjust policies or structures, or anyone in distress." Deacons may also assume other duties assigned by the session, including assisting with the Lord's Supper (W-3.0414).

In many congregations, this ministry is facilitated by dividing the church membership into zones (often along geographical lines), with one deacon responsible for each zone. In such cases, each deacon is asked to maintain contact with the individuals and families within his or her assigned area to confirm that they are attending church regularly; to make sure they understand the ongoing mission, goals, and objectives of the congregation; and to determine whether there are any outstanding needs that the church can or should address. In some cases, it means nothing more than making a phone call to keep in touch and to listen to concerns or complaints about the church. On occasion, it requires a personal visit or lunch together to share and discuss matters that are of a deep personal nature to the member. Often people are reluctant to reveal their problems to relatives, neighbors, and friends, and it may be that the deacons or the pastors are the only ones they dare trust. Occasionally when situations are really tough, deacons may be asked to provide critical advice (consulting with the pastor or other professionals first if necessary) and to recommend the name of a physician, financial advisor, attorney, accountant, pastoral counselor, psychotherapist, or psychiatrist. Because this last responsibility is difficult and somewhat frightening for some leaders, the board of deacons often includes regular training sessions in its meetings that are led by medical, mental health, or legal experts. In this way, deacons can feel prepared for any eventuality when they meet with members of the congregation.

In some churches, the deacons also work independently or with the Evangelism or New Member committees to help welcome new people into the church. One of the most common complaints visitors have about any congregation is "I went to church last Sunday and not one person greeted me." The deacons can help church members find organized ways to meet and greet visitors and make them feel welcome in the church family. Whether they come because they have just moved into the area, are looking for a new church home, are seeking to renew their faith in Jesus Christ, or are searching for God and for Christian fellowship for the very first time, a friendly greeting, a genuine desire to know a new person, and a careful follow-up can help visitors know that they are in a place where caring and love really are the top priorities. Active members may forget how important this personal contact is. On one occasion a woman who had served for two years as a deacon expressed anger at a deacons' meeting that people had still not made the effort to get to know her. When she expressed this concern after worship one day, some long-standing members objected, saying, "Don't we say 'hello' to you every Sunday?" Looking at them sternly, she said, "Yes, you do. But do you know what my name is?" The silence expressed their embarrassment at superficial friendliness in the church.

Deacons may also function as the stewardship committee in some churches, or they may work with the session committee assigned the duty of challenging the congregation to share and pledge their time, talents, and income at the time of the annual stewardship drive.

Deacons, of course, often take on many other ministries of sympathy and service. In some congregations, the deacons serve as ushers to greet all members when they attend worship. They work with the ruling elders and pastors to serve the Lord's Supper on a regular basis. They may act as lay readers or liturgical assistants during the worship services.

Deacons may be the ones who organize prayer chains through which members pray for one another in times of crisis or opportunity. They may also work with the Christian Education committee or with the Adult Education program to provide classes that introduce members to service opportunities in the church and the community.

The board of deacons may also be in charge of sending annual "care packages" to college students away from home for the first time. Individual members of the board may be assigned the responsibility of keeping in touch on a regular basis with all college and seminary students and with members in the military.

In many congregations, direct assistance to senior citizens is part of the deacon portfolio. Deacons provide monthly visits to shut-ins or members who cannot regularly attend worship services. Some churches also host monthly or quarterly dinners or luncheons for older members so they may enjoy fellowship together and benefit from Bible study and other programs of interest. The deacons may offer transportation to all church events for those who cannot drive and organize rides for members requiring regular visits to doctors and dentists or hospital treatment. Dinners are often brought to families who have loved ones who are ill or have passed away.

Sometimes the deacons institute free home-repair service staffed by volunteers from the church. For people who are elderly or on a limited budget, it is very comforting to know that someone they can trust is on call to help with plumbing and electrical repairs or that members are willing to assist with small painting and decorating jobs.

Deacons may run a community food shelf in cooperation with the other ecumenical or interfaith organizations, provide meals and housing for the homeless, organize advocacy programs for those in trouble with the law, or offer ministry to those in jails and prisons. The possibilities are nearly infinite. Wherever men, women, and children are in need of the healing presence of Jesus Christ, Presbyterian deacons can be there, limited only by their own creativity and their spiritual and financial resources. The last chapter of this book provides further suggestions regarding other exciting possibilities for ministry in the twenty-first century.

Qualifications

Deacons are ordained leaders in the church, and it is important that members with sufficient personal spiritual maturity and experience in the local congregation be elected to such an important position. The board of deacons is not a training ground for new members or an introduction to the Christian faith for new Christians. As we have seen in chapter 1, the author of 1 Tim. 3:8–13 makes it clear that those chosen must have impeccable qualifications and be of the highest moral character. The requirements are daunting:

> Deacons . . . must be serious, not double-tongued, not indulging in much wine, not greedy for money; they must hold fast to the mystery of the faith with a clear conscience. And let them first be tested; then, if they prove themselves blameless, let them serve as deacons. Women likewise must be serious, not slanderers, but temperate, faithful in all things. Let deacons be married

only once, and let them manage their children and their households well; for those who serve well as deacons gain a good standing for themselves and great boldness in the faith that is in Christ Jesus.

The *Book of Order* summarizes these qualities: "The ministry of deacon as set forth in Scripture is one of compassion, witness, and service, sharing in the love of Jesus Christ. . . . Persons of spiritual character, honest repute, exemplary lives, brotherly and sisterly love, sincere compassion, and sound judgment should be chosen for this ministry" (G-2.0201).

According to 1 Timothy, deacons are to keep in mind how important their work is and not treat it frivolously.

1. **Serious** (*semnous* in Greek) is an adjective that refers to people who are honorable, dignified, respectable, even religious or holy (in the sense of being set aside for service). The advice given in Titus 2:2 applies: "Tell the older men to be temperate, serious, prudent, and sound in faith, in love, and in endurance." Since deacons are often called upon to share the most intimate moments of members' lives, especially when they may be vulnerable and in a state of crisis, they must conduct themselves with sincerity and respect. They should remember that as ordained leaders they not only represent the local congregation and the Presbyterian Church (U.S.A.), but also follow in the footsteps of Jesus Christ (1 Pet. 2:21; Acts 20:35; 1 Cor. 11:1; 1 Tim. 1:16) and serve as his ambassadors to the community (2 Cor.

5:20). What they do provides an example to younger members and to those outside the church, and their actions must always adhere to the highest standards. "Set the believers an example in speech and conduct, in love, in faith, in purity" (1 Tim. 4:12).

2. **Double-tongued** (*dilogous*, literally "double-speaking," talking out of two sides of your mouth; cf. "double-minded" in James 1:8; 4:8) warns against the temptation to be two-faced in our witness, to say one thing to one group in the church and another to a second constituency, just to get along. Deacons must be honest in their witness to Jesus Christ and forthright in giving their opinions. "Show yourself in all respects a model of good works, and in your teaching show integrity, gravity, and sound speech that cannot be censured" (Titus 2:7–8).

3. **Not greedy for money** is a spiritual quality difficult for most Americans to claim for themselves since the temptation to want more and more things and to work night and day for material benefits is nearly overwhelming in our society. Yet scriptural guidelines urge us to make sure that we center ourselves correctly—to remember that our hearts will be where our treasure is (Matt. 6:21), that the love of money truly is the root of all evil (1 Tim. 6:10; Heb. 13:5), and that primary concern about investments and possessions will do more than choke out the growth of the Word of God in us (Mark 4:18–19) but will also make it nearly impossible to serve the poor who have virtually nothing in comparison with our great wealth. No wonder, then, that

the Directory for Worship declares that "the practices of stewardship and self-offering are a grateful response to God's love for the world and self-giving in Jesus Christ. As Christians, we are called to lives of simplicity, generosity, hospitality, compassion, and care for creation" (W-5.0103, also see F-2.05). Church leaders are expected to pledge their time, treasure, and talents to the church and thus provide positive examples for other members.

The warning about being greedy for money implies another obvious thing: church leaders must always be honest in their personal and business dealings, not to mention in their handling of church funds. Contracts must be put out to bid in the proper manner, workers must not be paid under the table, tax laws for nonprofit organizations must be observed, all funds should be properly audited, and church leaders must not pay kickbacks to contractors or look for ways to pad insurance claims. As Jesus puts it, "Whoever is faithful in a very little is faithful also in much; and whoever is dishonest in a very little is dishonest also in much. If then you have not been faithful with the dishonest wealth [*mammon* in the RSV], who will entrust to you the true riches? And if you have not been faithful with what belongs to another, who will give you what is your own?" (Luke 16:10–12).

4. **Not indulging in much wine** indicates that it will be hard for deacons to work with other members of the church who have personal and spiritual problems if they themselves are overwhelmed with physical or drug addictions or

compulsive personality traits. Although most Presbyterians are not teetotalers—and there is nothing wrong with having a good time—it should be remembered that is difficult to trust someone who has a drinking problem or appears to have one, even if it is understood that alcoholism is a serious illness rather than a sin. Church leaders and pastors should go to almost any length to avoid giving the wrong impression in the ministry of Jesus Christ. They need to realize that it is not a good idea even to have a single drink before going to a church meeting or making a home visit. People can get the wrong impression, rumors can start, and the ministry of Jesus Christ can be damaged and compromised (see Prov. 20:1; 23:29–35; Eph. 5:18–20).

5. **Hold fast to the mystery of the faith with a clear conscience** probably means that deacons should be men and women who understand the fundamental tenets of the Christian faith (Jesus as Lord; the meaning of his birth, teaching, death, and resurrection; following him as disciples; the significance of the sacraments; the authority of Scripture as the "witness without parallel (Confession of 1967, C-9.27), the meaning of witnessing and working for justice, etc.) without considerable reservations. In the PC(USA), as will be seen in chapter 4, all leaders are required to "sincerely receive and adopt the essential tenets of the Reformed faith as expressed in the confessions of our church as authentic and reliable expositions of what Scripture leads us to believe and do" (W-4.0404c). It is

also necessary to have a sense of wonder about what God does for us in Jesus Christ and not take it for granted. As Jesus speaks about "the secret [*mysterion* in Greek] of the kingdom of God" (Mark 4:12), and Paul concludes Romans with a reference to "the revelation of the mystery that was kept secret for long ages but is now disclosed" (Rom. 16:25–26), the author of 1 Timothy reminds deacons and bishops how awesome our God is and how "the mystery of our religion is great" since Jesus "was revealed in flesh, vindicated in spirit, seen by angels, proclaimed among Gentiles, believed in throughout the world, taken up in glory" (1 Tim. 3:16).

6. **Manage their children and their households well** is a requirement not just for women who may happen to be deacons or take on other leadership positions in the church but is demanded of all those who seek high office in the church. As 1 Tim. 3:4–5 points out, a bishop "must manage his own household well, keeping his children submissive and respectful in every way—for if someone does not know how to manage his own household, how can he take care of God's church?" It only makes sense. Even though church leaders are normal parents and have problems raising children, they cannot be so distracted with concerns that they are forced to ignore their duties to the family of the church. It is difficult, furthermore, for those who are anxious about the upbringing of their teenagers or the soundness of their marriage to pay sufficient attention to the needs of others.[6]

When deacons are nominated, due consideration must be given to the way they conduct their lives at home.

Following these and other scriptural guidelines, it is clear that the expectations for church leaders are high. They are carefully summarized in the *Book of Order*: "To those called to exercise special functions in the church—deacons, ruling elders, and ministers of the Word and Sacrament—God gives suitable gifts for their various duties. In addition to possessing the necessary gifts and abilities, natural and acquired, those who undertake particular ministries should be persons of strong faith, dedicated discipleship, and love of Jesus Christ as Savior and Lord. Their manner of life should be a demonstration of the Christian gospel in the church and in the world" (G-2.0104).

Term of Office

Once church leaders are elected and ordained, they remain ordained even if they are not currently serving on the session or the board of deacons. Although they cannot serve more than six years without a break of one year, ruling elders and deacons normally retain office throughout their

---

6. **Let deacons be married only once**: it should be noted here, of course, that we have a different expectation in regard to divorce and remarriage than the author of 1 Timothy. Although we take marriage and the maintenance of significant relationships with utmost seriousness, Presbyterians no longer remove members from office if they have been divorced, and they are not denied the right to serve if they have previously been married (F-1.0403).

lives. "Once ordained and while they are active members of any congregation of this denomination, ruling elders or deacons not in active service on a session or board of deacons continue to bear the responsibilities of the ministry to which they have been ordained" (G-2.0404). Most congregations are filled with ordained deacons and ruling elders who have served in the past, and the number can easily grow as new people join the church who were ordained elsewhere.

In fact, our Constitution takes ordination so seriously that it is not easy for a ruling elder or deacon to be removed from ordered ministry. Only three possibilities exist:

1. A deacon or ruling elder may be terminated when the church leader, after consultation and appropriate notice, persists in work that is disapproved by the session. If the ruling elder or deacon is warned that certain activities are judged to be harmful to the church, unethical, or divisive, the session can meet with him or her and require a change in behavior. If the leader refuses to listen and persists in acting in unacceptable ways, the session may assume that he or she has renounced the ordered ministry, and the clerk will report the renunciation at the next stated meeting (G-2.0407). Before such an action is undertaken, it would be wise for the moderator and the clerk of session to consult with the presbytery Committee on Ministry and the stated clerk to make sure that constitutional procedures and due process have been followed.

2. It is also possible, according to the Rules of Discipline, for charges to be brought against a deacon or ruling elder in a disciplinary case if he or she is considered to be guilty of an *offense*. An offense is defined as "any act or omission by a member or a person in an ordered ministry of the church that is contrary to the Scriptures or the Constitution of the Presbyterian Church (U.S.A.)" (D-2.0203b). If charges are brought, a trial must be conducted, an investigation made within carefully prescribed guidelines, and a judgment must be rendered by the session (see D-10.0000–11.0000). Possible degrees of church censure include rebuke, rebuke with supervised rehabilitation, temporary exclusion from ordered ministry, and removal from ordination (D-12.0101). The results may be appealed to the appropriate bodies at a presbytery, synod, and General Assembly level (D.13.0000). Again it is important to have appropriate consultations beforehand with the presbytery Committee on Ministry and the stated clerk.

3. It is possible, of course, for deacons or ruling elders to resign from the board of deacons or session whenever they consider it prudent themselves. If they do so for personal reasons (family illness, a new job, moving to another area, etc., G-2.0405), or because they sense that their presence as a leader is no longer a happy or productive one (due to conflicts in the church, for example), their ordination is not altered. Leaders may also resign if their belief system changes and they have, in their own judgment, departed from the essentials of Reformed faith and polity or if they

feel bound by conscience and their understanding of the Word of God to seek a new church or a new denomination. If they file what is called a "renunciation of jurisdiction," that is, if they claim in writing that they no longer want to be a part of the Presbyterian Church (U.S.A.), the session will remove them from church membership and the exercise of ordered ministry (G-2.0407).

Obviously it is a big step for anyone to decide that he or she wants to leave a congregation or a denomination to which the individual has given a great deal of time, energy, and love in the past. It is possible, however, that situations may develop in which conscience will not allow the continuation of relationships no matter how important they are. All those in ordered ministry take a vow (see the discussion in the next chapter) to further the peace, unity, and purity of the church, and when that seems impossible or when it appears that one can no longer provide a positive influence in the church, it may be time to move on to another place where one's talents and belief systems are better appreciated or more compatible.

Questions for Study and Reflection

1. Why did you decide to become a deacon when the nominating committee of your congregation contacted you? What talents do you have that especially qualify you to become a deacon?

2. Take a look at Rom. 12:3–21 and 1 Cor. 12:4–31 about the gifts of the Spirit. Which ones do you have? Can you identify gifts that are possessed by other members of the board of deacons? How do they all fit together as you do the work of the one body of Christ?

3. Call a nearby Presbyterian church or get the name and phone number of another congregation like yours in the presbytery. Find out what the tasks and responsibilities of their board of deacons are. Do their activities give you any new ideas? Would you want to meet with them sometime to compare your ministries?

4. What kind of training could you use the most on your board of deacons? Is there any way you could include mission education as part of your regular meeting? Would it help your board to have your presbytery sponsor meetings of deacons in your area to share opportunities and frustrations?

Chapter 4

Ordination Questions

*P*resbyterian deacons, ruling elders, and ministers are asked a series of questions at the time of ordination and/or installation (G-2.0403; 2.0704). Although most of them are identical, elders and deacons each take one unique vow to signify commitment to their particular calling. Ordination is an act by which the local church (in the case of ruling elders and deacons) or the presbytery (for ministers) sets apart persons to be presbyters or deacons called to perform special services in the church or in the world (see G-2.0701). It is carried out during worship as ruling elders and ministers perform the traditional rite of the laying on of hands to symbolize blessing and the passing on of authority and responsibility (see Gen. 48:14–20; Num. 27:22–23; Acts 8:17, 19; 13:3; 19:5–7; 2 Tim. 1:6; Heb. 6:2). The order of the service of worship is in W-4.04.

Question a

Do you trust in Jesus Christ your Savior, acknowledge him Lord of all and Head of the Church, and through him believe in one God, Father, Son, and Holy Spirit?

All ordained to ordered ministry publicly state their belief in Jesus as Lord and confess that it is only through him that their sin is forgiven (Rom. 10:9–13). By answering affirmatively, they accept the concept of the Trinity, one God in three persons.

Question b

Do you accept the Scriptures of the Old and New Testaments to be, by the Holy Spirit, the unique and authoritative witness to Jesus Christ in the Church universal, and God's Word to you?

A promise is given that new leaders will use the Bible, containing the revealed Word of God, as the primary guideline for everything they do inside and outside the church. As the Confession of 1967 puts it, "The Scriptures are not a witness among others, but the witness without parallel" (C-9.27). Although the Bible is the fundamental source for Christian decision making, it must be approached with literary, textual, historical, and archaeological understanding if it is to be used correctly as a guide for the church.

Question c

Do you sincerely receive and adopt the essential tenets of the Reformed faith as expressed in the confessions of our church as authentic and reliable expositions of what Scripture leads us to believe and do, and will you be instructed and led by those confessions as you lead the people of God?

Presbyterians are part of the Reformed tradition of theology and practice that started with Martin Luther, John Calvin, and John Knox in the sixteenth century when they and other Protestants "protested"against the Roman Catholic Church. As defined in our Constitution, "The Notes of the Reformed Church" include:

> the Word of God is truly preached and heard,
> the Sacraments are rightly administered,
> ecclesiastical discipline is uprightly ministered
> (F-1.0303).

Question d

Will you fulfill your ministry in obedience to Jesus Christ, under the authority of Scripture, and be continually guided by our confessions?

This question summarizes the two that preceded it and reiterates the commitment of those in ordered ministry to the lordship of Christ and the witness of the Bible. The confessions that guide them are found in Part I of our Constitution, the *Book of Confessions*, and are summarized in the next chapter.

Question e

Will you be governed by our church's polity, and will you abide by its discipline? Will you be a friend among your colleagues in ministry, working with them, subject to the ordering of God's Word and Spirit?

Presbyterians support a constitution with a history that extends back to the Protestant Reformation. Parts of the *Book of Order* were written in 1788 and 1797 (Historic Principles of Church Order, Historic Principles of Presbyterian Government, F-3.01; F-3.02). Our polity calls for the acknowledgment that God alone is the Lord of conscience, that we govern ourselves by majority rule, that "the Holy Scriptures are the only rule of faith and manners," that appeals can be carried from lower to higher governing bodies, and that they can be decided finally by the voice of the whole church in the General Assembly.

Question f

Will you in our own life seek to follow the Lord Jesus Christ, love your neighbors, and work for the reconciliation of the world?

Leaders in ordained ministry take a vow to do more than work for Jesus Christ when they are in the church. They also promise to serve him in their own personal lives in the way they conduct themselves in the community. They also make a commitment to recognize the value of the worldwide body of Christ and to support the church universal in its ministries of evangelism, healing, cooperation in mission around the world, and peacemaking.

Question g

Do you promise to further the peace, unity, and purity of the church?

Leaders in ordained ministry are obligated to work for the peace of Christ in the local church and in the presbytery, synod, and General Assembly. Their ministry is to be prayerfully pursued so that their presence may not be divisive but unifying. Although Presbyterians cannot possibly agree about the many issues that come before them, they are sworn to enter a discussion or debate in such a way that truth, Christian friendship, and the will of God are preserved. The "purity of the church" points to the tenets of Reformed theology and our desire to maintain them in our service to the church.

Question h

Will you pray for and seek to serve the people with energy, intelligence, imagination, and love?

The last general question for leaders in ordained ministry and pastors focuses on the qualities that they need to bring to the church, with God's help. Energy is required to overcome inertia in the congregation, to encourage the members and other leaders, and to get things done. Imagination assists in designing goals for the future, for discerning the will of God in prayer, and for daring to imagine new opportunities with the best creative gifts we have to offer in areas of worship, education, evangelism, and mission. According to the New Testament, love is the greatest gift of the Holy Spirit (1 Cor. 13:8–13); it is the first of the fruits of the Spirit (Gal. 5:22). Love is the best gift leaders can bring to the church, and the need for it never ends.

Question i (2)

(For deacon) Will you be a faithful deacon, teaching charity, urging concern, and directing the people's help to the friendless and those in need, and in your ministry will you try to show the love and justice of Jesus Christ? (W-4.0404i (2))

Like Question i (1) before it (for ruling elders), this one is just for one set of leaders. It concentrates on the fundamental duties of a deacon in the church. Deacons have a teaching role in the congregation, primarily by their words and actions in providing a role model of how love (charity) can be lived out in the community and the world. Charity is not a sop given to those in need to keep them quiet, but is action that comes from the heart to assist the poor, the homeless, those suffering from addiction or bad fortune, reaching out in the compassion of Christ to those who need us.

The work of a deacon, indeed of any Christian, does not have to be perfect. But we must "try" with the power God gives us to be like Jesus Christ our Lord.

Questions for Study and Reflection

1. How do vows you take in the church compare to those promises you make elsewhere, such as marriage vows or

the Pledge of Allegiance? Are they more or less important or serious?

2. Should a deacon affirm the ordination vows if he or she does not agree with all of them?

3. Which of the vows are the most critical for deacons today?

4. What should happen if deacons inadvertently break their vows? What should happen if they deliberately break them?

Chapter 5

Book of Confessions

All deacons, ruling elders, and teaching elders in the Presbyterian Church (U.S.A.) take a vow when they are ordained or installed (W-4.0404c) that they will adopt the essential tenets of the Reformed faith as expressed in the confessions of the church and that they will be led by these confessions as they lead the people of God.

In our church we are not directed by one confession but by twelve historic documents found in the first part of our Constitution, the *Book of Confessions.* Presbyterians believe that having several statements of faith rather than just one demonstrates the fact that confessions are dated and limited and that it is necessary for new ones to be written on occasion to express the Christian faith for a new time and place. We understand that the church is reformed, and always reforming: "The church reformed, always to be reformed according to the Word of God in the power of the Spirit" (F-2.02). The process for amending the *Book of Confessions* is outlined in G-6.03.

Confessions are subordinate standards in the church. That means that they do not replace the authority of Jesus Christ or the Scriptures that bear witness to him (F-2.02). Nevertheless, they are still valuable to us because through them the church proclaims to members and to the world who and what it is, what it believes, and what it resolves to do (F-2.01).

A brief summary of each historic statement in the *Book of Confessions* follows. Examination begins with the last one written in order to demonstrate the most recent confessional position taken by our denomination.

A Brief Statement of Faith (1991)

A Brief Statement of Faith was adopted by the General Assembly in 1991 in response to the reuniting of the Presbyterian Church U.S. and the United Presbyterian Church U.S.A. in 1983. Our most recent confession, it uses inclusive language throughout (except in the Doxology, where it returns to traditional Trinitarian wording).

The Statement takes up themes of particular interest to the church at the end of the twentieth century and in the beginning of the twenty-first century: Christology (the nature of Jesus, fully human and divine); ecojustice (linking environmental concerns with justice for all people, especially the poor); and spirituality (the need for the Holy Spirit in a broken and fearful world).

The Confession of Belhar (1982)

The Belhar Confession was written in South Africa in Afrikaans in 1982 and adopted as a statement of faith by the Dutch Reformed Mission Church in 1986. It was added to the *Book of Confessions* by the General Assembly in the PC(USA) in 2016. It rejected the long-standing heretical position of the white Dutch Reformed Church, which used the Bible in an attempt to validate its acceptance of the doctrine of apartheid.

The Confession of 1967

In 1956 an overture was sent to the General Assembly requesting a rewording of the Westminster Shorter Catechism. Later a special committee was appointed to write a new, brief, contemporary confession of faith.

The resulting statement of faith was outstanding in many ways: written at a time when Americans were deeply divided by racial conflict, the war in Vietnam, and sexual and economic struggles, the Confession of 1967 called for reconciliation for all people through Jesus Christ as Lord.

This confession also articulated a perspective of the Bible that differed significantly from the standards adopted by the Westminster Assembly in 1647. Acknowledging that the Scriptures were "the witness without parallel," the new statement clearly defined the necessity of using modern critical methods of exegesis for correct interpretation and called for an understanding of the cultural and sociological background of the biblical writers.

The Theological Declaration of Barmen (1934)

This important confession was written in direct response to the rise of National Socialism in Germany under Adolf Hitler. Meeting in Barmen-Wuppertal in May 1934, pastors and laypeople from the Lutheran, Reformed, and United churches courageously opposed the oppressive and deadly policies of the Third Reich. Declaring that all evangelical churches in Germany were imperiled by the teaching methods and actions of the official German (Nazi) church, the signers agreed that there was only one true leader (Führer) in Germany, and that he was Jesus Christ the Lord. They rejected the false doctrines that the State should become the single and totalitarian order of human life, or that the Church of Christ should be an organ of the State.

The Westminster Standards (1643–1647)

The goal of the Westminster Assembly was to reform the Church of England and reunite all the Reformed churches in Britain. Although it was composed mostly of English

Presbyterians, the Assembly also included Episcopalians, Presbyterians from Scotland, Erastians (Christians who wanted the state to rule the church), and commissioners from the Reformed Church of France.

The Assembly produced a number of confessional, liturgical, and organizational documents, and three of them have been included in the *Book of Confessions*. The Larger Catechism (questions and answers about the Christian faith) was written for preaching, and the Shorter Catechism was used for the instruction of children. Its most well known work, the Westminster Confession of Faith, was arranged around four themes: the Holy Scripture, the lordship and sovereignty of God, the covenant, and the Christian life. It remained the primary confession for most Presbyterians in the United States until the Confession of 1967 was adopted.

The Second Helvetic Confession (1561)

This long confession was written by the pastor who succeeded Huldrych Zwingli, the great Swiss leader of the Reformation. When Zwingli died, Heinrich Bullinger followed him in the pulpit in Zurich. The confession was originally written to be attached to his last will and testament since Bullinger did not expect to survive the plague that was sweeping the city. It became a public document when he sent it to Frederick the Elector, who needed a theological statement in his defense against charges of heresy.

Containing thirty chapters, the document begins with a statement about the nature of the Holy Scripture and its interpretation in church councils; it also deals with traditional concerns about the Trinity, the person of Jesus Christ, the concepts of the providence of God, justification by faith, the duties of ministries, and the definitions of the sacraments. It concludes with an exposition of the relationship between the church and state, an interpretation that influenced the Reformed church for years to come. The confession repeatedly rejects positions taken by other churches and sects that oppose Reformed traditions of theology and practice.

The Heidelberg Catechism (1563)

This catechism is organized into fifty-two units so that it may be used each Sunday for preaching. Written by Zacharias Ursinus and Kaspar Olevianus in 1562 at the request of Frederick III of Germany, it focuses on three points:

- Man's Misery, Man's Redemption, and Thankfulness
- The Trinity, the Apostles' Creed, and the Sacraments
- The Ten Commandments, Prayer, and the Lord's Prayer

In many Reformed churches throughout the world, including those in the United States, the Heidelberg Catechism is still used as the basis of weekly sermons. The tradition of using a catechism for teaching children and new believers also continues in the Reformed tradition. In 1998, the 210th General Assembly approved a new Presbyterian Catechism (The Study Catechism) for the instruction of all age groups in the church and for use in educational, home, and liturgical settings.

A new translation of the Heidelberg Confession has been approved by the required number of presbyteries. It must still be passed and enacted by the 221st General Assembly (2014).

The Scots Confession (1560)

Written at the end of a bloody civil war in England and Scotland between Roman Catholics and Protestants, the Scots Confession was written in four days by John Knox and five other clergymen. Approved by the new Scottish Parliament in 1560, it contains the fundamental tenets of the Reformed faith (see F-1.0303): the sovereignty of God; the election of God's people for service and salvation; justification by faith alone; the marks of the true church; the right administration of the sacraments; the interpretation of the Bible by the plain meaning of Scripture and the rule of love. It remained the theological standard for the Church of Scotland for nearly ninety years, until the publication of the Westminster Standards (1647).

The Apostles' Creed

Parts of the Apostles' Creed are clearly found throughout the New Testament where the church first expresses its faith in Trinitarian terms, in belief in the Father, Son, and Holy Spirit (Matt. 28:19; Mark 8:29; Rom. 1:3–7; 1 Cor. 8:6; 12:3; 15:3–7; 2 Cor. 13:13; Phil. 2:6–11; 1 John 4:2–6; 5:5). Similar statements are found in the writings of second-century Christians as well, but the creed as a whole did not appear in the form we recognize until the ninth century. Many congregations still use it as a regular part of worship as they confess their most fundamental beliefs about the nature of God, the origin of the universe, salvation, the work of the Spirit in the church, and the life to come.

The Nicene Creed (AD 325)

The oldest creed in the *Book of Confessions* is well known throughout the worldwide church and is often used in worship to express the faith of ecumenism. The Presbyterian Church (U.S.A.) uses two different versions: a translation based on the traditional text, and a newer, contemporary version approved by the General Assembly and a majority of the presbyteries in 1999.

The creed was written during a time of tense debate in the church during the fourth century, when disagreement existed about the person and nature of Jesus Christ. Although some Christians thought that Jesus was only "like" God and was not always fully the Son of God (the Arian controversy), it was decided at a church council at Nicaea (southwest of present-day Istanbul) that Jesus was indeed always God in every sense and was God from the beginning ("the only-begotten Son of God, begotten of the Father before all worlds, God of God, Light of Light, Very God of Very God, begotten, not made"). The traditional version we use today was approved at a second council in 381.

That the debate in the fourth century was important is clear to believers in the twenty-first century since questions about the person of Jesus persist, and Presbyterians still find it necessary to assert, as the General Assembly did in 2001 and 2002, that the concept of Jesus as Lord is still key for Reformed theology and practice.

The *Book of Confessions* is not a static document. The creeds and confessions "claim the truth of the Gospel at those points where their authors perceived that truth to be at risk. They are the result of prayer, thought, and experience within a living tradition. They appeal to the universal truth of the Gospel while expressing that truth within the social and cultural assumptions of their time" (F-2.01). Confessions can be added in the years ahead. As new issues arise, as different circumstances force Presbyterians to rethink their beliefs and the way the church is governed, the Constitution provides a way in which amendments may be made to confessional documents (G-6.0000) in order to continue as a reformed and reforming church. Recently, although the General Assembly approved the inclusion of the Belmar Confession, it was not supported by a sufficient number of Presbyterians.

Questions for Study and Reflection

1. Can you appreciate the need for having more than one confession? Does it bother you that the confessions may occasionally take different positions about Christian beliefs and actions? How would you explain the idea of having a book of confessions to someone who is not a Presbyterian?

2. The word *confess* means "to say the same thing," "acknowledge," "proclaim publicly," not "express repentance." How do you think this definition relates to 1 John 4:15, "God abides in those who confess that Jesus is the Son of God, and they abide in God"?

3. If we were going to attempt to write a new confession today, what would the key elements be? What would be the most controversial aspects? Do you think that Presbyterians could agree about the wording of a confession or creed for a new century?

4. Which confession or creed is the most important, in your opinion, for deacons in today's church?

Chapter 6

The Call for Creative Diaconal Ministry in the Twenty-First Century and Beyond

As the PC(USA) and other Protestant churches search for new ways to witness to Jesus Christ and serve him in the future, no one can be sure what forms ministry will take. Over the last few decades, the Presbyterian church has seen dramatic membership loss. Some congregations are in communities in the midst of economic downturn, and the prospects of growing (or even surviving) are uncertain. Yet in other small towns, suburbs, and city centers, Presbyterian churches are thriving, young families are looking for exciting new ministries, and great experiments are being developed to reach members and unchurched neighbors in dramatic and unexpected ways.

In the future to which God is leading us, it is not hard to imagine that ministries developed by deacons will need to be flexible and creative if they are to have a positive impact on the church and the society in which they are found.

1. Many small congregations are finding themselves in situations where they cannot afford to pay the salary and benefits for full-time pastors. Churches with a bigger membership base may have larger budgets and more affluent donors, but they too may suffer from a staff shortage. The cost of a second associate pastor, a full-time Christian education director, or a youth director may be too high. Many churches are finding it necessary to reduce pastoral ministry to half or quarter time. Seminary students are often beginning their studies later in life, and the length of their ministries is necessarily shorter than those who began just out of college. What will happen to the recruitment of pastors in the next fifty years is hard to tell, but it should be clear that for some churches to survive or provide the kind of ministries members need and deserve, it will be necessary for deacons and ruling elders to become more active in taking on the roles currently reserved for ordained clergy. The PC(USA) currently fills some of this gap by commissioning ruling elders to particular pastoral services (G-2.1001), allowing them to serve in a ministry validiated by the presbytery. Nevertheless, times ahead may call for deacons to take on more of the pastoral visitation of the church, the administration of the sacraments, and financial administration. Having lay leaders assume more of these responsibilities could become crucial in remote areas where pastors serve far-ranging yoked parishes or in congregations that simply cannot afford minimum salaries required by the presbytery.

In some congregations, deacons may find it advantageous to work more closely with the Stephen Ministers, who already have extensive training in pastoral care. It may also be possible to cooperate with other nearby Presbyterian churches to develop a unified diaconal ministry for several congregations. Responsibilities could be shared, and the needs of all members over a wide area could be more easily met.

2. In an age that is becoming increasingly wired—communication is nearly instantaneous, and information that used to take months to acquire can be retrieved in minutes on a home computer, a tablet, a smart phone, an iPhone, or even a wristwatch—the deacons may have to learn how to work with the session to utilize all the advantages of the Internet (Facebook, Twitter, YouTube, Flickr, etc.) to communicate with members and outsiders. The deacons can learn how to keep in touch with members needing pastoral care through e-mail and instant messaging as well as by texting. Opportunities for service in the church and the community can regularly be displayed on the church's home page on the Internet. Sermons and services of worship can be recorded and placed on a Web site or on Facebook or can be e-mailed to interested members each week to be played on the video players that come with home computers. Internet courses or classes on public access cable channels can be developed with other Presbyterian churches or nearby ecumenical or interfaith religious partners to help the community address critical issues of justice in their own areas. The deacons could help set up a

daily devotional Web site or sponsor a spiritual chatroom for interested parishioners. Many religious groups are now sponsoring online virtual worship centers in which people enter a digital worship space together and join in prayers, hymns, and selected Scriptures from current lectionary readings.

3. The board of deacons in the future can take the lead to offer comfort to the afflicted in new ways, especially by keeping abreast of changing programs in federal, state, and local social services and providing advocacy and help to those who find these systems bewildering or unresponsive. When state and federal agencies are forced to curtail their services because of changes in political policies or because of economic fluctuations, the church can work with other private agencies to raise money to continue or create programs to help those affected. Churches may find it necessary to take a more active role in providing adequate housing for the unemployed, people in low-income brackets, or elderly people whose retirement incomes are below a decent standard of living. Deacons could be instrumental in developing volunteer groups consisting of physicians, nurses, mental health experts, attorneys, accountants, and others who would be willing to help families and individuals who do not know where to turn when they are overwhelmed by medical, emotional, and financial problems. Churches can continue to provide necessary child-care and latch-key programs for single parents or for families in which both parents are forced to work to make a living. Deacons could also be

instrumental in helping their congregations establish much-needed services for those suffering from various addictions.

4. In the last two chapters of her thoughtful work on the nature of *diakonia,* Elsie Anne McKee emphasizes the need for deacons in the future to do more than extend pastoral care in new ways to the congregation and community: they must also lead the church in justice and caring ministries. Knowing that God in Christ calls us all to work for the justice of all the children of God (virtually anyone who is treated unfairly), McKee urges Christians in the Reformed tradition to recognize and deal with problems of discrimination. She also encourages believers to resist bias in the community, work to educate people about necessary political and social change, and challenge neighbors to support the religious and civil rights of all people around them. Service of God, she suggests, can be risky business as well as healing work, and the prophetic challenge that deacons can bring to the world of the future may help Christians develop a broadening vision that reaches beyond anything they can currently see or remember.[7] The General Assembly, for example, recently approved "An Invitation to Peace Discernment" for 2012–2014, which invites congregations and presbyterians to reflect particularly on the multiple wars that have taken place throughout the world and consider what it would mean for us to call ourselves a "peace church."

7. *Diakonia in the Classical Reformed Tradition and Today*, esp. 108–109, 112.

5. In 1992 the 204th General Assembly approved a study by the Task Force on the *Theology and Practice of Ordination to Office in the Presbyterian Church (U.S.A.)* that similarly challenges those engaging in diaconal ministry in the future to expand their vision to new horizons. Some of the guidelines for expanded service can be mentioned briefly.

• ***Exhibiting within the church and before the world the exemplary moral authority of sympathy, witness, and service after the example of Jesus Christ:*** Recognizing that the body of Christ can work to break down legal, political, ecclesiastical, and financial barriers that are often set up between people, the study urges the church to take on the pattern of Jesus' self-giving service. By consciously providing models of sacrificial service inside and outside the church, deacons can encourage others to adopt patterns of behavior that can work to bring the kingdom of God to realization in our world.

• ***Caring for the needs of God's people in crisis:*** The church's diaconal service can open up its ministry of sympathy to all people who are going through any kind of crisis in their private lives, in their marriages, in parenting, in jobs, in retirement, in sickness, and in health. In the 1990s, churches spontaneously organized to help communities ravaged by hurricanes, ice storms, and the horror of church burnings. After the events of September 11, 2001, congregations actively searched for ways to assist the families of victims, and they reached out to police officers and firefighters caught in the horror of terrorist attacks. In the future, boards of deacons can intentionally organize response teams of volunteers who are trained beforehand to help at home and abroad when the cup of cold water is desperately needed by God's children anywhere. In 2008 many churches reached out with financial assistance to those who lost their investments and jobs, and in 2011 help was given to those that faced the devastation caused by Hurricane Irene. Recently we have also seen how many lives have been lost and how many communities have been damaged through gun violence. What would it mean in the future for deacons to initiate studies of violence and work with other organizations to make their own towns or cities safer places to live?

• *Challenging structures and conditions, within the church and within wider society, which keep persons and groups powerless and voiceless:* Deacons are called not only to engage in ministries that attract the general approval of the church and society, but to afflict the comfortable, to challenge the conditions that lead to inequality and poverty in our lives, to look for ways to root out injustice and oppression, and to become the light on the lamp stand that illumines dark and hidden places. "In a broken and fearful world the Spirit gives us courage to pray without ceasing, to witness among all peoples to Jesus Christ as Lord and Savior, to unmask idolatries in Church and culture, to hear the voices of peoples long silenced, and to work with others for justice, freedom, and peace" (A Brief Statement of Faith, C-10, 65-71).

• *Becoming liturgical representatives of the church's presence in the world and the world's presence in the church:* Although Calvin was properly critical of churches that had reduced the service of deacons merely to roles as liturgical or administrative assistants, the 204th General Assembly encouraged Presbyterians to recover the central importance of deacons in worship and prayer. Deacons can especially participate in sections of the weekly service of worship where the ministry of service to the world is involved. Although other leaders and members are also welcome to lead the congregation in worship, the participation of the deacons in the reading of the gospel, the offering of the people's gifts, the prayers of intercession for the church and the community, and the preparing and serving of the Lord's Supper continually remind believers that all Christians are committed to leaving the sanctuary and following Jesus in vital ministries of compassion, witness, and service.

• *Developing new forms of leadership at every level of church, community, and governing body life:* Deacons can model new ways in which Presbyterians can work together at session, presbytery, synod, and General Assembly levels to serve the world. In particular, they can work to assist the homeless; refugees fleeing from terrorism and war; the hungry, abandoned children; and those with AIDS and other debilitating diseases, among others in need. Deacons can take the lead in challenging community leaders to minister to those who are in crisis. They can help organize mission trips in this country and abroad, and they can commission church members to join organizations that provide help in evangelism, Christian education, medical care, the rebuilding of churches and schools in areas devastated by natural disasters and war, and assistance in the fight against racism and oppression.

As we consider the future, we quickly realize that diaconal ministry may not be as easy or comfortable as it was once considered to be. The surprising, challenging, and even life-threatening aspects of some avenues of service will force Presbyterians to recommit themselves to a renewed willingness to follow Jesus Christ wherever he leads us in his love for God's children and his search for justice. We will need to ask for courage, wisdom, and power from God as we reach out in love to the broken communities that surround us and to a world reeling from the painful effects of economic inequality, continuing racism, and the destruction and fear caused by vicious acts of terrorism.

With the passage of the new Form of Government in 2011 other possibilities for more flexibility in the ministry of deacons (and ruling elders) are made possible.[8]

---

8. See Earl S. Johnson, Jr., "New Flexibility in Church Administration," *Presbyterian Outlook*, May 2012. For some other ramifications, see the "Foreword to the Fourth Edition" and "Introduction," in *Presbyterian Polity for Church Leaders*" by Joan S. Gray and Joyce C. Tucker (Louisville, Ky.: Geneva Press, 2012).

Deacons may now be elected, for example, on staggered terms so that one class can work for a one- or two-year term in order to concentrate on a special ministry that calls for a period of more intense leadership (G-2.0404). If a congregation is too small to elect a board of deacons, furthermore, individual deacons may be ordained for specific tasks for which they have been trained such as a congregational visiting nurse, a teacher of Bible or theology, or a counselor or social worker who meets with parishioners (G-2.0202). In larger congregations a board of deacons could be expanded (say from twenty-four to thirty members) and have the additional deacons focus exclusively on new ministries or be "on loan" to small churches that need assistance in certain areas of ministry.[9]

In the future, we may need to develop new standards by which we judge success or failure. Perhaps in the coming years it will be more important to be creative, innovative, spontaneous, and Spirit-filled in our service than it will to be safe and orderly. In the days to come, it may not be easy to set and fulfill goals or plan ahead with certainty. In spite

---

9. For information about the role of deacons in some other denominations, see Marvin A. McMickle, *Deacons in Today's Black Baptist Church* (Valley Forge, Pa.: Judson Press, 2010); William Ditewig, *101 Questions and Answers on Deacons* (Mahwah, N.J.: Paulist Press, 2004); Benjamin L. Merkle, *40 Questions about Elders and Deacons* (Grand Rapids: Kregel Publications, 2007); Thabiti M. Anyabwile, *Finding Faithful Elders and Deacons (9 Marks)* (Wheaton, Ill.: Crossway, 2012). Find online resources for the United Methodist Church at "Deacons and Diaconal Ministry," http://www.gbhem.org/networking/deacons; for the Episcopal Church, The School for Deacons, http://www.sfd.edu/; for the Roman Catholic Church, "Bishop, Priest, and Deacon," http://www.catholic.com/tracts/bishop-priest-and-deacon.

of all that we do and say, an unknown future—whose shape may change radically before we even arrive—may force us back to the fundamental conviction that, regardless of our best efforts, what we need to do most, as the first ordination vow reminds us, is to trust in Jesus Christ. Then, as the last vow confirms, we need only *"try* [italics added] to show the love and justice of Jesus Christ," knowing that in the trusting and the trying lies our real power and our final success.[10]

Questions for Study and Reflection

1. How often does your board of deacons assess your goals and objectives? Do you have any responsibilities from the past that really do not serve the church or the community any more?

2. When was the last time that your board took on a new service project?

3. What ministry of compassion, witness, or service does your church really need right now? How about your community or presbytery? What is stopping your board of deacons from initiating it?

---

10. In 2013 I wrote several articles in *Presbyterian Outlook* encouraging congregations to study the gifts of the spirit as they plan for the future. The final one was "What Is the Spirit Saying to the Churches?" *Presbyterian Outlook,* November 25, 2013, 23.

4. What services do you think deacons will be called to give to your church in fifty years that are not being offered now?

5. Is your church involved in any programs that help alleviate poverty, racism, parochialism, or prejudice in your community? What else could you do?

Appendix

A Litany for the Recognition of Deacons

Leader: Loving God, hands have been laid upon the deacons here before you and they have answered your call to ministry. Enable them to have a ministry that is truly one of compassion, witness, and service.

Deacons: Our God, in the touch of friends and neighbors, through the voices of pastors and teachers, out of your presence in our hearts, we have responded to Christ's command to serve his body and the world he loves.

People: Let them be worthy of your trust in them; give them the strength to meet the challenges before them.

Leader: We pray that their work may truly be that of *compassion* for those whom they are asked to serve.

Deacons: Keep us from being condescending or merely concerned out of duty, but empower us to have genuine compassion and pathos, to share the feelings of others, to feel with the people of our church:

People: as we celebrate, rejoice, and laugh; as we struggle, weep, and grieve; as we mourn and agonize for the pain and sin of the world.

Leader: Let the congregation be blessed by the mercy they extend. Give them the mind of Christ that they may forgive not only those who hurt others out of ignorance but especially those who are enemies of justice and love and know precisely what they do.

Deacons: Sustain our inner beings with power through your Spirit, and let Christ dwell in our hearts through faith, as we are being rooted and grounded in love. Let us strive for harmony in and out of the church community. Let us be the ones who work to understand the roots of conflict and violence in the community and in the world. Give us the ability to be catalysts for Christ's love as we try to bring sisters and brothers back into the unity only you can provide.

People: O Living Word who communicates with us through the Incarnate One, help the deacons in their *witness* to proclaim Jesus Christ in all they say and do.

Deacons: In our preaching and teaching enable us be knowledgeable, Spirit-filled, cheerful in bringing good news, and true to you.

Leader: In their actions in the church and in society let them be known for concern for all people, for honesty and fairness, and for the ability to follow our Lord Jesus Christ.

Deacons: In our ministry give us power to heal the sick, comfort the lost, bind the broken-hearted, visit those in jail, and be courageous advocates for those who are forgotten or shunned by society.

Leader: O Christ who gave up everything for us, even life itself, make it possible for all of us to give ourselves in *service,*

People: to surrender all to God, so that denying ourselves, we may be able to reach out to the spiritual centers of those around us.

Leader: In a world that powerfully tempts us to sell our souls for power, material benefits, recognition, and popularity,

People: give us the wisdom to be servants who want most of all to be rid of everything that prevents us from focusing on what you want us to do.

Leader: Help us to remember that our neighbors are anyone we find in need, that we never dare pass by on the other side, that no one you have created can be considered ugly or useless by us or unworthy of our concern or care.

Deacons: Prevent us from taking for granted the gifts of the Spirit we have. Let us hone and practice them until they are energized to full power.

Leader: And where we are weak let us remember to ask for the fruit of the Spirit that you offer to all who need or want them:

People: when we are discouraged, give us joy;

Leader: when we are angry or hateful, give us the peacefulness and the ability to make peace that only come from the One who is our peace;

Deacons: when we are in a hurry and want to push those who cannot change, give us endurance and patience that trusts in you;

People: when we are mean, kindness;

Leader: when we are selfish and self-serving, generosity;

People: when we doubt or are afraid, faithfulness;

Deacons: when we are too demanding and rough, gentleness;

People: when we are wild with passion or want to satisfy only ourselves, self-control;

Leader: and above all, give us the love from you that constantly amazes us and passes all our understanding,

All: the sharing, responsive love that thinks more of others even than of self.

Leader: O Jesus Christ, Holy One, set apart to serve all God's children,

Deacons: let us be worthy of serving you;

All: and in everything we do and say let us follow in your footsteps, our Savior, Lord, and Master, our example, mentor, guide, and friend. In your name we pray. Amen.

Glossary

Book of Confessions. Approved by the General Assembly in 1967, it contains eleven historic statements of Reformed faith that guide the church in its study and interpretation of the Scriptures. It directs the church in maintaining sound doctrines and equips it in its work of preaching and teaching (F-2.01).

Book of Order. Based on the experience of Presbyterians since the seventeenth century, it consists of the Foundations of Presbyterian Polity, the Form of Government, the Directory for Worship, and the Rules of Discipline; it contains directions and recommendations for the governing of the church on all levels.

confession. A statement in which the church publicly declares what it believes and intends to do (F-2.01).

Constitution. The Constitution of the PC(USA) consists of two parts: the *Book of Confessions* and the *Book of Order* (F-2.01; F-3.01).

creed. A short statement of faith beginning with a personal reference ("I believe . . ." or "We believe . . .").

diaconal. Having to do with the New Testament concept of service; the work of the deacons and other members of the Christian church.

elders. Leaders of the church elected by the congregation. Together with the ministers of the church, they exercise leadership, government, and discipline in the church. The word *elder* comes from the Greek word *presbuteros* and means a wise person or one who is older. Ruling elders currently in active service make up the session of the church. Teaching elders are now called ministers or pastors.

laying on of hands. A ritual of blessing used in the Old Testament and New Testament; utilized in the modern church in ordination services for new deacons, ruling elders, and ministers.

offense. "Any act or omission by a member or officer of the church contrary to the Scriptures or the Constitution . . ." (D-2.0203b).

ordered ministry. Includes men and women called by God through the church, deacons, ruling elders, and teaching elders to exercise special functions according to their gifts (G-2.01).

PCUS. The Presbyterian Church in the United States, often called "the southern church." It was reunited with the UPCUSA in 1983 after separation at the beginning of the Civil War.

session. The ruling body of the church, consisting of ruling elders who are currently elected to serve.

UPCUSA. The United Presbyterian Church in the United States of America, often called "the northern church." It was reunited with the PCUS in 1983 after separation at the beginning of the Civil War.

For Further Study

Basic Resources

Angell, James W. *How to Spell Presbyterian.* Rev. ed. Louisville, Ky.: Geneva Press, 2002.

Beattie, Frank A. *Companion to the Constitution: Polity for Church Officers.* 4th ed. Louisville, Ky.: Geneva Press, 1996.

Boyd, Lois A. and R. Douglas Brackenridge. *Presbyterian Women in America: Two Centuries of a Quest for Status.* 2nd ed. Westport, Conn.: Greenwood Press, 1996.

Chapman, William E. *History and Theology in the Book of Order: Blood on Every Page.* Louisville, Ky.: Witherspoon Press, 1999.

Gambrell, David. *Presbyterian Worship: Questions and Answers.* Louisville, Ky.: Westminster John Knox Press, 2019.

Gray, Joan S. and Joyce C. Tucker. *Presbyterian Polity for Church Leaders.* 4th ed. Louisville, Ky.: Westminster John Knox Press, 2012.

Johnson, Earl S. Jr. *Selected to Serve: A Guide for Church*

Leaders. Revised for the new form of government. Louisville, Ky.: Westminster John Knox Press, 2012.

————. *Witness without Parallel, Eight Biblical Texts That Make Us Presbyterian*. Louisville, Ky.: Geneva Press, 2003.

Parsons, Gradye. *Our Connectional Church: The Hopeful Future of the PC(USA)*. Louisville, Ky.: Westminster John Knox Press, 2018.

Shedd, Charlie W. *The Pastoral Ministry of Church Officers*. 7th printing. Atlanta: John Knox Press, 1974.

"Theology and Practice of Ordination in the Presbyterian Church (U.S.A.)." Approved by the 204th General Assembly, 1992. In *Selected Theological Statements of the Presbyterian Church (U.S.A.) General Assemblies (1956–1998)*. Louisville, Ky.: Presbyterian Church (U.S.A.), 1998, 568-616. For reference to the "Office of Deacon" see 601–16.

Manuals

Simmers, Marvin, ed. *Consider Your Ministry: A Study Manual for New Officers*. 5th ed. Louisville, Ky.: Presbyterian Publishing House, 1993, PDS #60002.

Venerable, William H. *Your Job as a Church Officer: A Manual for Officers of the Local Church*. 3d ed. Pittsburgh: Rivertree Christian Ministries, 1998.

Witherspoon, Eugene D. Jr. and Marvin Simmers, eds. *Called to Serve: A Workbook for Training Nominating Committees and Church Officers*. Louisville, Ky.: Curriculum Publishing, Presbyterian Church (U.S.A.), 1997, PDS #500129.

Studies of the Ordination Questions
and the *Book of Confessions*

Burgess, John P. *Confessing Our Faith: The Book of Confessions for Church Leaders*. Louisville, Ky.: Westminster John Knox Press, 2018.

Dowey, Edward J. *A Commentary on the Confession of 1967 and an Introduction to the Book of Confessions*. Philadelphia: Westminster Press, 1968.

Eberts, Harry W. Jr. *We Believe: A Study of the Book of Confessions for Church Officers*. Philadelphia: Geneva Press, 1987.

Janssen, Allan J. *Confessing the Faith Today: A Fresh Look at the Belgic Confession*. Eugene, Or: Wipf and Stock Publishers, 2018.

Johnson, Earl S. Jr. "The Confession of 1967: Fifty Years and Counting." *Presbyterian Outlook*, November 29, 2017.

———. *Selected to Serve: A Guide for Church Leaders*. Revised for the new form of government. Louisville, Ky.: Westminster John Knox Press, 2012.

Rice, Howard and Calvin Chinn. *The Ordination Questions: A Study Guide for Church Officers*. Louisville: Ky.: Presbyterian Publishing House, 1993, PDS #060003.

Rogers, Jack. *Presbyterian Creeds: A Guide to the Book of Confessions*. Louisville, Ky.: Westminster John Knox Press, 1991.

———. *Reading the Bible and the Confessions: The Presbyterian Way*. Louisville, Ky.: Geneva Press, 1999.

The Study Catechism, Full Version with Biblical References. Louisville, Ky.: Presbyterians for Renewal, 1998.

For Advanced Study

Beyer, Hermann W. "δiakoneō, diakonia, diakonos." In *Theological Dictionary of the New Testament. Vol. 2.* Edited by Geoffrey W. Bromiley. Grand Rapids: Wm. B. Eerdmans Publishing Co., 1964.

Blake, Eugene Carson, ed. *Presbyterian Law for the Local Church: A Handbook for Church Officers and Members.* Published for the Office of the General Assembly by the Publication Division of the Board of Christian Education, 1953.

Calvin, John. *Institutes of the Christian Religion.* Edited by John T. McNeill, translated by Ford Lewis Battles. Philadelphia: Westminster Press, 1960.

Loetscher, Lefferts A. *A Brief History of the Presbyterians.* Rev. and enld. Philadelphia: Westminster Press, 1958.

McKee, Elsie Anne. *Diakonia in the Classical Reformed Tradition and Today.* Grand Rapids: W. B. Eerdmans Publishing Co. 1989.

Smylie, James H. *A Brief History of the Presbyterians.* Louisville, Ky.: Geneva Press, 1996, 112-13.

Zigmund, Barbara Brown. "Ministry of Word and Sacrament: Women and Changing Understandings of Ordination." In *The Presbyterian Predicament: Six Perspectives.* Edited by Milton J. Coalter, John M. Mulder, and Louis B.Weeks. Louisville, Ky.: Westminster/John Knox Press, 1990, 134–58.